LEADING

WITH VISION

LEADING

WITH VISION

...in real estate and in life

Carlos Redmond

ISBN 0-9759543-1-8
Deutsch & Deluca Publishing LLC
Las Vegas, NV

CONTENTS

DON'T STOP WITH SUCCESS... THINK BIGGEST
V. STAY ON FIRE
VI. PUSH YOUR BOUNDARIES

LEADING

WITH VISION

Leading with vision...
and finishing dreams

To achieve great success in real estate investing requires a subtle balance between vision and reality. You need to see the possibilities in every situation, but you also must learn to work with the hand you're dealt.

The top real estate investors know when to be bold and take risks. They also know when to walk away. And they understand the value of finishing other people's dreams.

To become truly successful in real estate investing – to become a leading investor – you need a go-for-broke mentality. You have to be willing to jump in and make mistakes. You will never reach the next level of success if you don't. Just be sure you don't make the same mistakes twice. Always be learning. Always be improving.

Laziness, ego, insecurity, greed – these are the traits of novice investors that will never make it big. Confidence, focus, patience, hunger – these are the traits that will set you on the road to success.

Learn the subtleties along the way:

- The need to plan ahead is often accompanied by the need to change course.

- The ability to delegate is enhanced by the ability to retain control.

- Diversification doesn't mean a lack of focus.

- The smallest projects are often as lucrative as the largest, and sometimes more so.

- Conquering adversity doesn't open the door to carelessness.

- Success doesn't happen overnight – but it's important to accept a good opportunity when one appears.

- Innovation doesn't mean everything has to change.

What might seem at first like contradictions are in fact a balance of skills and approaches that distinguish the most successful real estate investors from those that will never reach the top. If you can understand and practice these skills in balance, you have the potential to become a leader – in real estate investing and in life. You will have the ingredients for incredible success.

Perhaps the most important subtle balance of all is the one most real estate investors miss: Leading with vision doesn't mean ignoring the opportunity to finish someone else's dream. If there's one key to significant success as a real estate investor, this is it.

Anyone can start a project and flame out in the middle. Very few can step in and bring that project to completion. It should be the easiest, most obvious step to take. Ego prevents it. You don't always have to be the one with the great ideas. You just have to know a great opportunity when you see one.

THINK BIG...
AND
STAY ON
TARGET

You won't go far in real estate investing without confidence and focus. You have to be willing to go for broke – backed up by confidence in your due diligence. Don't be distracted by doubts. Don't second-guess yourself into trouble. Believe that you'll succeed, even when you experience setbacks.

No matter how solid your plans and how detailed your analysis, things go wrong. It's important that you know when to walk away, when to look for alternatives and when to accept your mistakes, learn from them and move on.

Experience is the key to your success as a real estate investor, and you won't acquire the experience you need unless you're willing to take some calculated risks and losses. Train yourself not to panic when things go wrong. Every deal moves you forward.

In real estate investing, success is a long-term endeavor. The more you're willing to jump in and try new types of investments, the closer you'll move toward your goals… and the bigger your goals will become.

I. BE CONFIDENT

1

Be willing to go broke.
For the right reasons.

No real estate investor ever made serious money by being afraid to go broke. Scared money doesn't earn money. You might show a small profit on a few transactions, but you'll never make the big money – half a million a year or more of profit – unless you are willing to stick your neck out.

Every time you go for broke, you gain something. If the situation works out well, you'll gain money. If the transaction doesn't go well, you'll gain knowledge of what not to do the next time. Don't underestimate the value of that knowledge. It will put you far ahead of those who don't take a chance. Unless you go for broke, you won't gain the experience that will pay off in the long run –

regardless of how the immediate transaction turns out. Go for broke, and in one way or another, you'll win every time.

How do you gain the courage to go for broke? It's based partly on mindset and partly on common sense. Mindset: You must be committed to significant long-term success and the belief each investment will pay off in some way, even when you lose money. Common sense: You must know better than to gamble with money you need to pay the rent or put food on the table.

Going for broke doesn't mean just tossing money into the air and saying, "Whatever happens, happens." It doesn't mean acting carelessly or foolishly. Rather, it's a success mentality grounded in thorough research and analysis of every real estate transaction you enter. Going for broke means covering all bases and hiring the best experts to help you.

If you don't pay for the best attorneys and accountants, for example, going for broke will be too much of a risk. You need the best people working for you so you can be confident going into every transaction. You're not just paying for hours of time or paperwork. You're paying for experience. You're paying to avoid future mistakes. The best attorneys and accountants have learned over time what can go wrong. Having their expertise in your corner will prevent a lot of headaches. Besides, if a transaction goes bad, you'll have to pay to hire an attorney or accountant anyway. Why not pay them up front, so things will go well instead?

As long as you know what you're getting into with each transaction, as long as you minimize your risk by doing thorough research, you won't be tempted to second-guess yourself. That will put you one step ahead of most new investors. Too many times, people start forward with a deal and then pull the plug at the last minute, because they start having doubts. You'll cause more trouble for yourself that way than if you just go for broke and see it through.

Be willing to go for broke. You might lose a few times, but as long as you're careful and focused, you'll gain in the long run.

2

Know your limits.

Don't be constrained.

In real estate investing, a go-for-broke mentality means always seeing the possibilities... seeing beyond your limits. Without it, you'll never get ahead. At the same time, you have to live in the real world. You need to be realistic about every deal you become involved in. You have to know you limits.

Knowing your limits doesn't mean being constrained. Too many people use their limits as an excuse not to succeed. They hold back, believing they lack the knowledge or the means for significant success. This is amateur thinking. To become a leader in real estate investing, you need to learn how to move ahead despite your limits. How to make the most of what you have.

What if you need to buy 10 new homes to build your portfolio, but you aren't certain that you should buy all 10 at once? Should you limit yourself to just a few homes?

Why should you limit yourself? Look at the situation more closely. If you can find two homes that will close earlier than the other eight, and they all require only $1,000 of earnest money up front, there's a very good chance that by the time the other eight close, your profit on the first two will allow you to pay for the others. If not, you've lost nothing but a few thousand dollars in earnest money.

Don't let a great deal pass you by just because you don't have quite what you need to complete it. Find a way to make it work. Sometimes this means finding a partner.

If you want to start a restaurant franchise that requires a certain amount of money, which you have, and a certain amount of restaurant experience, which you don't have, you can partner with someone who does. Or if you have no money to close on a house but you know you'll earn $80,000 in profit, find someone who has the money to go in on it with you. You do all the work, and they provide the cash. In each case, you'll split the profit with your partner, but 50% of something is better than 100% of nothing.

It all comes down to ambitious plans and a realistic way to get there. This requires creative thinking, looking at all avenues to success. To become a leading real estate investor, you must have a realistic knowledge of what you can and can't do. But don't let that keep you from reaching your goals. Find a way to move ahead despite your limitations, and you will be well on your way to success.

3

Don't fear adversity. Plan for it.

How many Chicken Littles do you know? You'll meet plenty in real estate investing. The sky is always falling for these people. They'll never get ahead. When you focus on the worst that can happen, it usually does. Your fears become a self-fulfilling prophecy, because you don't allow yourself the confidence to go for broke and reap huge rewards.

Don't become a Chicken Little that focuses only on the downside. Be realistic, knowing the downside exists, but don't always think it has to involve you. Remember that for everything that can go wrong, there is plenty that can go right. Why not picture yourself on the winning side for a change?

When you dwell on problems, they're always bigger in your mind than in reality. This is especially true in real estate investing. You keep worrying about "What happens if?" Then when things go right and you're ready to cash your check, you kick yourself and wish you'd done more. Guess what? If you hadn't spent so much time worrying, you *could* have done more.

You have to watch your mentality going into every project – and coming out of every project too. A successful investor is not just someone who can jump into the right deals. It's also the person who can recover quickly from deals that go wrong.

You think you're going to sell a property to someone and at the last minute, the person says, "No." This panics so many investors, and it shouldn't. You should be able to walk away and move on to the next transaction. Whatever goes wrong, you should be ready to learn from it, so you can experience greater success in the future.

The way you react to adversity depends on how well prepared you are. When you conduct due diligence and focus on the details, you limit what can go wrong – and you limit the chance you'll be caught completely off-guard when something does go wrong. You'll be ready to assess the situation calmly and learn whatever you need to learn so the next transaction goes more smoothly.

Whenever an investment doesn't go as planned, keep the big picture in mind. Remind yourself this isn't your only deal. You'll move straight into the next deal and make up for your loss. That's much more productive than stewing over what went wrong. If you don't maintain the right attitude and you allow one loss to become more important than your next gain, you'll miss opportunities. In real estate investing, you should always be ready to move on to the next profitable deal – no matter what preceded it.

It helps if you don't put all your eggs in the same basket. You should always work on several deals at once, and have the next one ready to go the moment your current transaction is completed. I knew an investor once who only wanted to focus on one deal at a time. I never understood why. He always had several potential projects lined up, all of them good, but he ignored the rest while he waited for the first one to go through.

What if there was a delay? Real estate transactions are complex and involve several parties. The timing of the transaction won't be as important to all parties. If you're waiting for an action from the city or county government, for example, they might not proceed as quickly as you anticipate. Why delay your chance to earn a profit?

If you have multiple deals going, you'll always have another deal to work on when you encounter a problem with one.

Working on multiple deals will also help you avoid the temptation to rush. Too many new investors want to get rich quick. That's not the path to long-term success in real estate investing. It's not about how quickly you earn money but how well you do it, and for how long. Focus on the details, and you'll minimize the chances that things will go wrong.

If you find a great price on a piece of land, for example, be sure the investment is sound. Inspect the property to be sure it's build-able. Check with the government to be sure the seller actually has the right to sell the land. Be sure there's no mold or other environmental hazards on the property, or your anticipated profit of thousands of dollars can turn into a very expensive liability.

Also confirm that you will have access to the land before you buy it. Some parcels of land are landlocked between others, and you won't have physical access to your own land without going through a long and costly process. The seller sometimes won't know this; they might have purchased the land for investment and aren't aware of the problems. You have to do thorough research to find out what you're really getting for the price you pay.

The same goes for financing. Just because someone give you a good interest rate, that doesn't mean the rate is fixed. I ran into an investor that thought he was getting a 2% fixed interest rate on a 30-year mortgage. The fixed rate, as it turned out, was only for one year. Beware of lenders chasing commission. You think they're trying to help you, but they're not. Check the details. Be sure you know what you're getting into.

If you conduct due diligence effectively, if you focus on multiple deals and if you react calmly and analytically when things go wrong, you'll be in the right frame of mind to deal with adversity. You'll have no reason to let fear of adversity hold you back from success.

4

Don't fear mistakes.

Learn from them.

Don't let fear of failing stop you from trying to succeed. It's not just a matter of having confidence to go forward despite adversity. You also need to learn not to analyze everything to death. Don't try to proceed with so much caution that you paralyze yourself. You will make mistakes – believe me, you will. But you will learn from them, and that's crucial.

To become a leading investor, you need to reach a level of confidence that can be acquired only through experience. This includes the experience of making mistakes. The more mistakes you make, because you try new types of investments and increasingly complex deals, the more prepared you'll be for higher-level transactions down the road. Without the experience forged through mistakes, you'll never reach that level, much less succeed when you get there. Don't fear mistakes. Learn from them.

Learning from your mistakes also means you don't let the same mistakes happen over and over. It never fails to amaze me how people keep spinning their wheels and running into the same problems again and again. Patience and perseverance are admirable qualities, and there's no such thing as overnight success in real estate investing. But if you keep running into the same problems over and over, that's a very clear signal you're doing something wrong. Take the time to figure out what it is. Learn from your mistakes.

If you're ready to sell a house and you discover at the last minute your buyer isn't qualified, you'll know that next time, you should pre-qualify your buyers. If you don't make this a requirement, and another buyer fails to qualify on a future sale, it's your own fault for not learning from your mistake.

I knew an investor who constantly drove clients around to properties, only to have them make low-ball offers that were always refused. Finally I told him, "Unless you want to continue to be a taxi driver, and a secretary who draws up contracts all day, only to have them all rejected, you'd better start educating your clients about the impact of a low-ball offer in a hot market." If he didn't sit down and have a talk with his clients, he would never close on one deal.

Too many people believe the exaggerated comments they hear; someone tells them they bought a house for $80,000 below market, when everyone knows that in a hot market, that's not likely to happen. But people insist on believing the myth, and they keep spinning their wheels, waiting for their low-ball offer to be accepted. If you are their broker, you'll be spinning your wheels too unless you manage your clients' expectations.

When the same problems come up again and again, figure out what's going wrong and do something to change the situation. If you make a mistake once, that's great. You'll gain valuable experience that will help you succeed down the road. If you make the same mistake twice, you're moving backward. Stop and figure out how to avoid that mistake in the future.

II. STAY FOCUSED

5

Have a plan.

Know when to drop it.

To achieve outstanding success in real estate investing – or any endeavor – you need to plan ahead. If you want to achieve a certain level of success by a certain date, you won't know what steps you need to take today unless you have a detailed plan that shows you how to get from here to there.

If your goal is to own 50 properties in 2008, for example, don't wait until 2007 to start buying them. Don't expect instant success. When you hit it big, people will think your success came overnight. You'll know better. Overnight success is really the result of a series of actions taken over a period of time. Instead of waiting for success to come to you, start moving toward it by following a detailed plan.

Don't let your plans limit you, however. They are meant to be a guide, not a straitjacket. Situations don't always work out the way you anticipate. You need to be able to think on your feet. Keep your larger goals in mind when you focus on details. If you find a different and better way to reach your larger goals, don't be afraid to change course. Don't allow yourself to become stuck. Have plans, but know when to drop them.

This applies to individual transactions as well as to your overall goals. If you're buying a piece of land, for example, be sure you have a plan for what you're going to do with the property. At the same time, if someone comes along and wants to do a joint venture, don't automatically say *No* just because it's not part of your plan. A fool answers without thinking. The same fool later asks himself over and over, "What if I said *Yes*?" Next thing you know, you're calling the other investor back, begging to be part of his joint venture. Now he has the advantage.

Be prepared to change course even when you've found the "ideal" situation. If it proves to be less than ideal, don't be stubborn. Walk away.

I was looking at a piece of commercial land once, and it was a great deal. The seller was asking $200,000 and I knew the property was easily worth $700,000. The trouble started when the seller's attorney stepped into the picture. He started insisting that we pay for subdividing and other expenses that would be nothing but a headache. I walked away from the deal.

You could look at this situation and say I walked out on an easy $500,000 that I would have earned within six months. But when the hassles started, there was no longer anything easy about the project. What if the seller changed his mind after I paid for subdividing? What if he found a way out of the contract? Meanwhile, my money might have been tied up for months while we sorted out the legalities. I knew there were other deals that would earn me just as much money. If I hadn't walked away from this one, I wouldn't have been able to take advantage of better opportunities.

I was negotiating on a restaurant franchise one time, and the person who wanted to go into the business with me couldn't qualify for a license. Even so, he wanted 60% of the profits, and he insisted on that right up front. We hadn't even started negotiations. He said he refused to share the risk – even though it was minimal – and when I asked for his profit goals, he had no answer. I knew right away that deal wouldn't work out. It was a great location and we would have made plenty of money, but it wasn't worth the hassle of dealing with an unreasonable partner for 10 years, which were the terms of the deal.

When hassles and headaches arise at the start of a transaction, that doesn't bode well for what might happen later on. Don't expect the other party's attitude to change. If you're having problems now, those problems will only get worse. Walk away. A broken engagement is always preferable to a broken marriage.

Don't be stuck with a plan that no longer works. If you're trying to earn $5 million a year, and you know the most you can earn selling properties is $2 million, don't fight it. Don't be stubborn and try to do the impossible with sales, just to prove you can. You'll miss too many good opportunities. Find another way to earn the other $3 million – land leases, a grocery store, a restaurant franchise. With real estate investing, there's always another way.

Have a goal. Have a plan that will take you to that goal. But be ready to play the hand you're dealt.

6

Diversify.

Do it well.

For a real estate investor, the only limits to success are those you create in your mind. Just because you do one type of investment well, don't think that's all you should focus on. You might earn a decent income that way, concentrating on one segment of the real estate market. But it's unlikely you'll achieve significant wealth unless you move into several different areas of real estate investing. Diversification has the added bonus of reducing risk: you spread your risk across several areas, put your eggs in different baskets.

Diversification is possible in many ways. You can cover a wide range of real estate investments or focus on a few types of investments in different markets. The sky is the limit – as long as you do each type of investment well and hire the best experts to support you. This means choosing your areas of concentration wisely. Focus on what you do best, and when those transactions start to work favorably and consistently, allow yourself to learn something new.

If you want a portfolio that includes new homes, high rises and land, for example, don't try to learn all three types of investment at once. You'll be mixing information and causing yourself all kinds of headaches. Don't spread yourself too thin by thinking you can do everything at once. Don't allow greed or ego to get in your way.

Learn the craft instead. When you can do one type of investment well, move on to the next. You'll have a better foundation, and you'll be able to invest at a higher level when you move on to the next area.

Too many individuals try to diversify by branching into completely new areas that involve more than just real estate transactions. They start getting involved in restaurant or café management. That's an entirely new market that requires dealing with employees and a host of management issues. When you try to diversify in that direction, you'll likely end up running the restaurant. Is that really what you want to do?

If you want to own a restaurant, why not own the building instead? Or purchase a hotel so you can diversify with a different type of commercial property. Hire a management company to run the property for you. That's the smart way for a real estate investor to diversify.

Other diversification possibilities include land leases. You purchase land and allow builders to put structures on it, through a long-term lease that often spans a 50- to 100-year term. Land can be a great way for a new home investor to diversify. You don't have to rush into land acquisition. Just start investigating until you become as knowledgeable with land as you are with new homes.

If you typically rent out houses, why not try to purchase a small apartment complex? Or perhaps try an RV park. With an RV park in the right location, you can receive $300-500 per month for one RV space. That's not a bad way to diversify your rental investments.

Plenty of diversification opportunities are available for real estate investors, without branching into other investment areas. Whenever and however you diversify, do it well. Focus on what works for you and what you do best.

7

Remember luck doesn't exist. Opportunity does.

Timing is everything in real estate investing. What appears to be luck is really a matter of timing. The desire to succeed meets the situation. Everything comes together.

This leads to strategy.

Look at the big players in each segment of the real estate market. Find out where they're involved and what they're doing. Learn to get in and out of those areas quickly, without attracting their attention.

If two big builders are squabbling over a 500-acre project, for example, and you can find a 5-acre piece of property nearby, go out and buy the property and then advertise. Maximize the opportunity – that piece of property would be useless if the big players weren't fighting over the bigger piece nearby.

Don't get in the middle of their fight, however. Don't let your ego get in the way; don't try to become what you're not. You're in this to make money, not to try and outdo the big builders. Get in and get out.

Just because luck doesn't exist, that doesn't mean fortunate opportunities won't open right in front of you. The problem most novice investors face is that they question every opportunity. They assume everything is too good to be true. They can have the sweetest deals right in front of them, but they refuse to take advantage of them. Instead, they sit there and think of all the reasons they shouldn't move forward.

These are the same people that come back later, after someone else has made a profit from their missed opportunity, and complain. If you were the one to introduce the opportunity to them, they will say, "Why didn't you tell me I should do this?" even though you told them many times. Be prepared for people who don't seize opportunities to come back and blame you. They always do. Just don't become one of those individuals.

It's wise to be cautious, but don't overanalyze. Don't throw away a good opportunity

8

Don't take egos seriously. Including your own.

You'll encounter many egos in real estate investing – individuals who have reached their first level of success and want you to know it. What you should recognize instead is that they will not likely advance any further. You will… if you learn to ignore them and not take their egos so seriously.

Don't react personally to everything people say to you. If you do, you show your weakness. People learn from that – they learn how to gain an advantage over you. They discover that if they keep pushing your buttons, you will keep reacting. You'll keep showing weakness. That's what they want, so they'll continue to do it. By reacting personally to their arrogance, you're just provoking them to greater egotistical heights.

Learn to throw them off balance instead. If they talk about the Bentley they're going to buy tomorrow, tell them you have two but you're thinking about getting a Rolls Royce. Take all the air out of their comments. They won't know whether or not you're being serious. You'll keep them off balance. They won't know what to expect.

For years Charles Barkley refused to acknowledge that Michael Jordan was a better player. It wasn't until Barkley retired that he admitted it. Why? Because it gave him an edge. He needed that edge to succeed. When you work consciously to deflate someone's ego, you give yourself an advantage that person would prefer to have over you. You have the edge.

Be careful not to go overboard, though. Don't act egotistical yourself. Nothing turns people off faster. Like the novice investor that walked into my office and, during the course of a conversation, asked one of my real estate specialists if she'd ever seen a deed to a house before. He was all hyped up because he had just purchased his first investment home. He tried to act like he was a seasoned pro. He failed – miserably.

It's great to act like a successful investor before you reach that level, because that helps you stay focused. You'll achieve more that way. But before you play the role, be sure you know how a successful investor acts. Surround yourself with them. Listen to what they say – and pay attention to what they don't say. That's the only way you will ever sound like a genuinely successful investor before you become one.

I was at a luxury car dealership one time when a couple of guys walked in trying to show off. They waved a bunch of cash around and tried to get the dealer to offer them a better price on the car they wanted.

"Are you kidding?" the dealer said. "Cash does nothing for me. It's all cash to us."

These guys thought carrying a wad of cash made them special. They thought they'd get a better deal, not to mention respect. Instead, they displayed their ignorance. Today cash is delivered instantly. It doesn't matter if you pay for a car by check or if you take out a loan. The dealer still receives instant cash. Because these two guys didn't take the time to realize that, they looked foolish.

Don't act the part unless you are a part of the cast. Otherwise people will jump at the chance to take you down. You'll just be putting yourself in the same class of investors that will never get ahead.

Take yourself seriously. Have the confidence you need to succeed and don't hesitate to show it. But don't fall into a battle of egos. Don't worry about what other investors think of you. Those whose opinions matter won't think about you at all. Those that get in your way – they don't matter. Just handle your investments well, keep moving up, and the over-inflated opinions of others will become irrelevant.

DON'T LET

YOUR

EGO

HOLD YOU BACK

As a real estate investor, nothing will stop your success in its tracks faster than your ego. I always know an amateur investor by the way the person's ego gets in the way of everything. Ego destroys your confidence and focus. Ego is distracting and misleading.

If you let your ego run your real estate investing business, you'll be trapped in unsuccessful negotiations and transactions you'd be better off avoiding. You'll burn bridges unnecessarily. You'll listen to the wrong people for the wrong reasons, and you'll ignore advice you should listen to. You'll miss great opportunities.

Ego will fool you into thinking you should do everything yourself, because you're better than everyone else. If you listen to your ego, you'll lose the benefit of teamwork and finishing other people's dreams. You'll become mired in mediocrity.

If you want to become a leading real estate investor, don't let your ego get in the way. Approach real estate investing intelligently, professionally and confidently. Learn to be better than your ego.

III. BE BETTER
THAN YOUR EGO

9

Listen to others' advice. Know when to ignore it.

Too many real estate investors fail because they don't know who to listen to and when. They let the wrong people tell them to hold back and be cautious when they should move ahead. They ignore excellent advice when they receive it. When they listen to the wrong people, it's because they lack confidence. When they ignore the right people, it's because their ego gets in the way.

If you want to succeed as a real estate investor, you have to learn to distinguish between good and bad advice. You need to realize everyone has something valuable to say – and it's worth listening to, even if you choose to ignore it.

I used to believe I shouldn't listen to people who don't have money, but that's not necessarily true. I've learned plenty from people who don't have money. They've taught me the importance of sticking to the basics. This is something people with money could never teach me. From people who don't have much money, I've also learned to appreciate every opportunity. Even the smallest deals can pay off big; I just have to do more of them.

Even though people without money have taught me valuable lessons, I've learned just as much from people with money. When I first started out as a real estate investor, I learned from the wealthiest people to shoot for the stars. Don't always be realistic. Aim high and you'll move a lot further than you would by aiming low.

Those who are wealthier than you and those who have less than you – each has something valuable to say, something worth listening to.

This doesn't mean you should follow the advice of everyone who has an opinion on what you're doing. You should listen to what they have to say, but then decide whether or not their advice is worth taking. Learn how to distinguish between a valid consideration that might affect your success, and a concern that's irrelevant and will only hold you back.

Plenty of people will offer advice – the more successful you become, the more compelled they will feel to contribute their two cents. Even if their advice is good, it might not fit your situation. Some people will urge caution when it's not warranted. They'll offer criticism when something isn't working, but they fail to see the big picture. Perhaps it looks on the surface as if something isn't working, but if they step back and look through your eyes, they'd see everything is falling into place.

When you become more involved in real estate investing, you'll hear from people, "Watch out for this person" or "Be careful: everyone is out to scam everyone else." While you should always proceed with caution in any real estate transaction, you won't go far if you are paranoid that everyone is out to get you. Learn to be cautious of the serpent but innocent like the dove.

When someone gives you advice about real estate, always consider where the advice comes from. Do they really understand what you're doing? Are they speaking from a limited point of view? Are their goals different from yours? If so, thank them for their opinions and then move ahead with your own plans. The same people who are critical of something you're doing today will later say they knew it would work out. Then they'll do exactly what you did.

I've run into that so many times. People are eager to tell me exactly why a particular type of real estate investment won't work. They'll give me excellent reasons why I shouldn't jump into the investment. While I consider their reasons to see if they apply to my situation, in most cases I discard them. When the transaction is successful, the same people come back and say, "We knew it would work." They change their story completely.

When you do decide to follow their advice and things don't work out, they'll say, "You didn't do exactly what I told you to do." Even though you did. Or they'll tell you that you were supposed to do something a particular way – which is the exact opposite of the way they told you to do it.

People will try to tell you, "That kind of investment never works. My Uncle Fred tried that, and he lost a fortune." Before you take their warning seriously, ask yourself what kind of investor Uncle Fred was. Did he have your background, your knowledge and training? Were the circumstances identical? Or was he someone that jumped into the deep end of the pool without knowing how to swim? In most cases, you'll realize quickly that Uncle Fred's situation was different from yours, and just because something didn't work for him, that doesn't mean you won't succeed. No one else can understand your circumstances as well as you do, and no one else can predict your future.

Before you decide to follow someone's advice, ask yourself if that person is successful in their own life, in their own field. Success has more to do with a person's approach than anything else. If someone is successful in their own area, that's a good indication they could also become successful in real estate investing, because they have the right approach to getting ahead. They have the negotiating savvy, organizational skills, ability to deal with the public, leadership qualities – everything it takes to do well in real estate investing. Their advice might be worth listening to – if it applies to your situation.

On the other hand, if the person isn't successful in their own field, keep that in mind before you take their advice seriously. If they've always gone bankrupt in every endeavor, or if they routinely blame their lack of success on others, that's not someone you want to accept advice from.

Take advice for what it's worth. Free advice is worth exactly what you paid for it. That doesn't mean you shouldn't listen. You should never be too big to listen to the opinions of others. Just don't believe everything you hear, and don't assume everyone else's advice always applies to you.

10

Negotiate for what you want. Don't waste time.

The ability to negotiate effectively is a great skill to have, in real estate investing and in any other type of business. If you can, take a negotiating class, the kind of class attorneys take. Learn different negotiating techniques, such as facial gestures and distractions that throw a person off balance. A negotiating class will teach you how to mask your feelings, so the party you're negotiating with might think you're unhappy, for example, when in reality you're very happy with the situation and just don't want them to know that.

If you have training in negotiations, you will always have an advantage in real estate transactions. If you tell someone you'll get back to them by 5:00 p.m., for example, and that person isn't skilled at negotiating, you'll have a distinct advantage when you call the person back at 4:57 p.m. Without the knowledge of how to negotiate effectively, that person has no doubt been waiting for your call all day. By not calling, you've put thoughts in the person's head. People always think the worst. When you don't call, they think the deal isn't going through. They spend all day sweating. By the time you do call, they'll be ready to agree to whatever you offer.

You also have to develop an awareness of other people's negotiating skills. You should always know who you're dealing with, in terms of their ability to negotiate. It's obvious right away when someone is not experienced. They'll act nervous or uncertain. They'll say, "Let me think about it" to everything you ask, or "Let me call you right back." That's your cue they aren't confident negotiators.

If, on the other hand, you're dealing with someone who appears to be a good actor, that person probably has very good negotiating skills. If you are trained in negotiating, you'll know how to respond. If you don't have negotiations training, that person will have an advantage over you. Negotiating basically comes down to who can put on the best act.

Sometimes you'll encounter a person that thinks they can negotiate but lacks formal training. They're self-taught. Be especially careful with this type of person. They don't know when to say *Yes* and when to say *No*. They're more likely to throw you off balance than anyone, and there's no logic behind it. If you really want a property and they say *No* to your very fair offer, just because they think they're being savvy, you might buckle under pressure. They'll make a mental note that this is the best tactic to use with you, and they'll start saying *No* to everything. That's a bad routine to fall into.

Before you jump into negotiations, know who you're dealing with.

It's not enough to know how to negotiate. You also need to know when to stop negotiating, when to walk away. You have to keep your bottom line in mind at all times and keep your emotions out of the transaction. Don't waste time fighting a losing battle. In real estate investing, there is never just one opportunity to earn a profit. Don't tie up all your energy negotiating a deal that isn't going your way.

For example, let's say there's a house in Naples, Florida you want to buy, and the house is selling for $500,000. You already know your bottom line price is $480,000. If the seller comes back to you with $483,000 as an acceptable price, that's close enough for you to take it. But what if they hold out for $500,000? No matter how much you want the property, you have to walk away at that figure. Don't return the call, don't continue the conversation, don't try to negotiate for a more acceptable price. Just make a clean break and walk away. Why? Because the more you discuss the property, the more you'll want it.

In many cases, when you walk away from a negotiation, the person will later come back to you when they realize they can't sell the property for their asking price. This happened to a friend of mine recently – not with real estate, but with an $80,000 watch he wanted to buy. He knew all he was willing to pay was $45,000. The sales person said, "No." My friend walked away. Later that day, the sales manager of the store called him and offered the watch for $50,000.

Know how to negotiate, know who you're negotiating with, and know when to walk away.

11

Mentor others.

Keep your priorities.

No matter how successful you become, don't ever think you're too good to help others. If someone needs a mentor, be willing to help them out. This doesn't mean you have to take the time to walk them through everything and give them a free ride. Most people just need a little direction or a few suggestions they can follow up. They need a starting point. Give them some advice, some direction, and that's more than enough to put them on the right track.

When you agree to mentor someone, don't attach strings. Don't expect anything in return. Mentoring is something you do because you want to give something back, in appreciation of your own success, or because you have particular knowledge or experience that will be helpful to someone else. Mentoring isn't about bartering. Don't expect the person you're mentoring to offer anything in exchange.

Don't get carried away with mentoring, however. To become a leading real estate investor, you need to remember what your time is worth. You can't spend all day mentoring people, or you will never move your business forward. You can't take time out in the middle of high-value transactions to hold someone's hand every time they take a step. Get them started, and that's it. Don't turn it into an ongoing coaching relationship. You can't afford the time or the energy.

Most people don't need that type of mentoring. Those who do are deliberately trying to get a free ride, whether consciously or unconsciously. They will suck all the energy out of you, and all for nothing, because they won't succeed even with your help. They don't have the enterprising spirit it takes to become a successful real estate investor. They will simply waste your time and theirs. When that type of person approaches you for advice, just give them one or two pointers and walk away.

If you learn how to value your time, you'll know right away when other people don't. Someone came to me once for help in real estate, and I gave him a few ideas. Next thing I knew, he sent a friend to me, asking that I qualify her for a mortgage on a house. She had no money and bad credit. It was impossible to qualify her, and I told him so. His reply: "I knew she wouldn't qualify, but I wanted her to hear it from a professional." What did his remark tell me? That he didn't value my time. Whenever he called me after that, I sent his calls to voice mail.

When I decide to mentor someone, that person has to catch my attention or be someone worth helping. I look for people eager to learn, people who can take my advice and run with it. People who need just a little direction. I steer clear of those that are trying to use me. I also know when to stop mentoring and focus on my own priorities.

At the end of the day, you're responsible for your own success. Your priorities come first. Don't let mentoring cause you to lose focus on what you need to do. Most times when you mentor someone, that person won't last as a real estate investor. They'll give up or change their mind and tell you, "I've decided I don't want to do that anymore." If you just spent a little time giving them pointers, it won't matter if they walk away. But if you've invested all your time and energy into teaching them how to invest in real estate and they decide to quit, that's a huge waste. You could have invested your time and energy toward your own success instead.

Mentoring is important. It's a way of acknowledging your appreciation for your own success by giving new investors a head start. But watch who you mentor and don't over-invest your time and energy. Keep your own priorities number one.

12

Create your own vision.
Be a dream finisher.

You can't become a leading real estate investor if you lack vision. To succeed in real estate investing, you have to be willing to go ahead with projects others might walk away from. You need to appreciate and focus on the big picture, even when others tell you that your immediate goals are impossible to achieve. You have to remind yourself that you see possibilities other people will never see.

Even so, your own vision isn't the only path to success. To become a truly successful real estate investor, you need to appreciate the vision of others. When another investor's idea has great potential, but for whatever reason that person can't see it through, be willing to step in. Become a dream finisher.

Nevada billionaire Kirk Kerkorian is a very successful dream finisher. When others run out of money, he steps in and builds what they couldn't. In Las Vegas, we have people that build hotels but they can never take it to the next level, because they run out of money. For every visionary that begins a project, there's someone with money and the ability to step in and finish that person's dream.

You don't have to operate on a grand scale to be a dream finisher. At every level of real estate investing, you'll find plenty of opportunities to finish someone else's dream. This requires vision of a different type: the ability to visualize someone else's goals and carry them through. People fail all the time in real estate, not because of bad ideas but because they run out of money. If you have money, their dream can lead to your success. They've already paved the way.

Unfortunately too many real estate investors will miss out on opportunities to become dream finishers. Why? Ego. They want the idea, the vision to be theirs, not someone else's. They don't want to pick up where someone else left off.

This is a foolish attitude and it will prevent you from becoming a leading investor. Learn to look for the best opportunities and build your success that way. Don't be trapped into thinking all the great ideas have to be your own.

What if you always wanted to build a first-class condo, but you never had the money? Someone else is building a beautiful condo nearby, and you find out they're out of money. They can't finish the project. Are you going to resent that person for starting what you were unable to start? Or will you see the situation for what it is: an opportunity for you to finish what they started?

You should always be ready to see a successful situation in a project someone else has started. Don't let your ego stand in your way of purchasing the property and taking over. You are finishing that person's dream, and the end result will bring your success. Rich people go broke all the time and have the perfect projects going. They just need someone to bail them out. If you are willing to step in, you can profit tremendously from what they've started.

While you're keeping an eye on your ego, watch out for jealousy too. Nothing gets in the way of your judgment faster than jealousy. A jealous mind clouds opportunities, makes them invisible. All you see is a person you envy or a project you resent. You fail to see that this person's project could become your key to success. What difference does it make if the other person started the project? If you finish it, the ultimate success will be yours. At the end of the day, when you succeed, disagreements, envy and resentment will be irrelevant. It's only your success that matters.

Jealousy can affect you on so many levels in real estate investing. It closes so many doors. Too often I've known investors to turn down great opportunities, simply because they had a personal grudge against the person inviting them. How will you get ahead if you make everything personal? Ego and emotions have no place in successful real estate investing.

What if another investor with an excellent program is hiring and asks you to join the team? Will you say *No* simply because you went to school together and you resent that this person has become successful more quickly than you? What difference does it make? Would you rather keep starving and missing great opportunities, or can you learn instead to put your ego on the shelf and seize the chance to do better? Join the team, and you'll be closer to experiencing your own success.

Besides, if you really think you're smarter or that you should be more successful than the other person, why should you be jealous?

Everyone's goals are different. Everyone pursues those goals differently. Just because others got a break before you did, that doesn't mean you won't become more successful than they are. Your circumstances are different and your approach is different. Don't judge them negatively just because they bring a great opportunity to your door. They're not trying to rub their success in your face. Most of the time, they will be completely unaware of your resentment. It's all in your head. So put the idea out of your head, jump in and take advantage of the opportunity.

To succeed in real estate investing, you need vision – your own, and the ability to complete another person's vision, to finish another person's dream.

IV. LEARN
TO DELEGATE

13

Learn to delegate tasks.
Be able to do them yourself.

You might have heard the saying, "Pay people well but not so well they don't need you; and teach them well but not so well you need them more than they need you." To succeed as a real estate investor, you should remember this advice.

Successful investing depends on your ability to delegate. You need a top-notch team working for you, even when you're starting out. An attorney, a CPA, a realtor, a mortgage lender – these will be your initial team members. By delegating tasks to them, you will move ahead more quickly than you would on your own. Let them do what they do best, so you can concentrate on what you do best. When everyone puts their unique talents to work, everyone wins.

If you want to become a leading investor, you need to take this a step further. Not overnight, but gradually you'll assemble a larger team, including people to help you do research, analysis and other types of legwork. This doesn't mean you'll hire a full-time staff, though you might decide that's the way to go. Or you might outsource all your needs instead. Either way, you'll need confidence in your ability to delegate.

You have to be able to trust others to do excellent work for you. This begins by hiring the best and making sure they are focused on your vision of success. When their success is connected to your own, they will become an asset to you. If they fall short, replace them. Everyone is replaceable – and you should make that clear right up front.

Delegating is a hard concept for many people to put into action. People who understand the theory of delegating can't bring themselves to do it. They want to be in control all the time. They want to handle everything themselves. The truth is, if you don't learn to delegate effectively, you're not in control of your business or your success. One person neither can nor should do everything. If you don't delegate, you will always be working with one hand tied behind your back. You will always be limited.

The problem stems from impatience, ego and greed. A person who doesn't want to delegate is usually reluctant for one or more of the following reasons: They want everything done now and they're afraid if they hire someone to do it, that person will be too slow; they want to prove to everyone they can do everything themselves; or they don't want to spend money hiring someone else.

Each of these reasons is flawed: If you hire the right people and train them properly, you don't need to worry they'll be too slow – and if they are, fire them; attempting to prove you can run a business single-handedly only signals to those who are truly successful that you're an amateur; and if you think you are saving money by doing everything yourself, think again.

If you need information quickly, do you pick up the phone and make a call? How are you going to build a successful real estate investing business if you do that? Your job is to do the work of a $1,600/hour executive, not to make a $3 phone call you could pay someone $15 an hour to make.

This might seem trivial – how long does one phone call really take? – but add up all the phone calls you make during the day, and you'll be amazed how much of your valuable time you waste. If you want to become a leading investor, you need to spend your time structuring multi-million dollar deals. If you start making exceptions – a phone call here and there – you will get into a bad habit and miss opportunities in the process. The world of real estate investing moves quickly. In the time it takes you to make one quick phone call, a window of opportunity will shut.

Don't ever hesitate to pay people, just because you think you could do the same job "for free." When you look at this from the perspective of a successful real estate investor, who can generate thousands of dollars worth of business in the time it takes to make a phone call anyone could make, you'll realize the trivial work isn't really free. It costs you the amount of money you might have earned in that time – and that's much more than it would have cost you to hire someone to make phone calls.

I can always identify a greedy individual or an amateur by the amount of work they try to do themselves. They don't know how to value their time. I know how to do land deals, for example, but often I give the commission to another realtor to help me out, because I'm busy working on bigger deals. I already know what I'm going to do with the land and I know how much profit I'll earn, so I have no problem paying an extra $6,000 to the realtor to help me. As one of my accountants likes to say, "You worry about making the money and I'll worry about how we keep it."

Even though you need to delegate, you also need to know how to do every aspect of the job yourself. In a dynamic industry such as real estate investing, change happens. Change is what drives your success. Learn not to fear it, but to be prepared for it. This means being ready and able to step in if one of your team members walks out. Even though you've delegated specific tasks to that person, you should be able to complete those tasks in a pinch if the person leaves.

Think about it. You're in the middle of a major transaction and one of your key team members chooses that moment to follow another career path. What will you do? Will you let the transaction fall apart because you either don't know how to do the job yourself, or because you think you're too big to do the job? Or will you step in as if nothing is amiss and complete the transaction successfully?

You don't ever want to put yourself in the position of having to beg a team member or an employee to stay. You don't ever want your real estate investment business to go under because you thought you were too big to make phone calls and do legwork to complete a transaction, when the person who was supposed to do the job decided to take off.

Every time I delegate a task to someone, I know how to do the job myself. I don't have time to do it – I should be spending my time earning more money and creating more opportunities for the business, not making phone calls I can pay someone to make. But if it ever became necessary, I could make those phone calls myself. I'd know who to call and what to ask. I've never asked someone else to perform a task I couldn't complete myself.

I can tell my assistant to talk to a VP of a restaurant chain, for example, and ask questions about certain locations, how much the franchise fee is, how much the build-out is, etc. I don't have time for that conversation, but I know exactly how the conversation will transpire. My assistant isn't forming a relationship and obtaining information I wouldn't be able to duplicate if necessary. When you delegate a job that requires legwork, it's important that you know how to do the legwork yourself.

It's also important that the person doing the job is aware that you could do the job too. In the example of calling the restaurant chain, my assistant would know I could make the same call, because I would tell her exactly what to ask. When she comes back to me with the answers, she'll know by my reaction she hasn't uncovered any information I didn't anticipate. Even if she tells me something

I didn't expect to hear, I won't act surprised. If I did, I'd be letting her know she could do something I couldn't.

To be a leader in real estate investing or in any other endeavor, learn to delegate. But know how to do the job yourself, just in case.

14

Don't micromanage.
Retain control.

Even when real estate investors finally learn to delegate, they have trouble giving up control. They give other people a job to do, but then they continue to micromanage, constantly looking over everyone's shoulder and focusing on every detail of the work others are doing for them. This is worse than not delegating in the first place, because you're paying others to do their jobs, but you're not letting them work. You're wasting time and money.

If you want to become a successful real estate investor, resist the temptation to become bogged down in the daily details of your business. Don't get caught up in trying to determine whether a $2 refund was credited to one of your vendor accounts, for example. In the time you spend trying to save $2, you'll be losing the $2,000 you might have earned if you concentrated on doing your job and let someone else worry about the invoice.

I knew an investor who lost out on a good opportunity because he kept trying to redo the work of the person he hired to help him. The situation was already set up and all he had to do was wire the money to purchase a new home. Instead, he tried to redo everything himself, wanting the deal to be structured his way, refusing to trust the work of the person he had hired.

At the end of the day, the deal he restructured was worse than the deal he had going in. He created so many new problems and became entangled in so many arguments that he missed by five minutes the deadline to wire the money. As a result, he lost the chance to buy the property – which turned out to be quite profitable for the investor who ultimately purchased it.

When you delegate, you put people in place to free up your time, so you can earn more money. These are people you selected, hired and trained. Trust your decisions. Don't ruin the arrangement by attempting to micromanage. Let your business run itself while you're out negotiating deals that will make your business grow.

How many times have you heard about a head of the family that passed away, and the family or household fell apart shortly afterward? That's because no one but the head of the household knew how to keep things running. No one else was trained. As a leader in real estate investing, you should never put your business in that position. If you were incapacitated – say you were laid up in the hospital for a week – would your business fall apart? If so, you're micromanaging too much. Your business should run successfully even in your absence

At the same, don't let your business run away from you. Everyone who works for you should realize they are not indispensable. They should be aware they are not doing anything you couldn't do yourself or find any number of replacements to do.

Does this contradict what I said about not micromanaging? Absolutely not. You can maintain control without constantly looking over everyone's shoulder. The top business leaders know how to do this. If you want to be a leader in real estate investing, you need to learn it too.

Set up a system of checks and reporting procedures: create mini-structures in your office that make people responsible to others. Hire an office manager, for example, to oversee everyone else's work and to give you a weekly productivity report. If the weekly report indicates something isn't going right, appoint your office manager to fix the problem. If problems continue, either find a new office manager or replace the person causing all the difficulties. This way, you stay in control, but all that's required is a few minutes of your time each week as you review the productivity report with your office manager.

It's also smart, especially when you have a new employee, to be sure your requests are translating correctly. You might put a person in charge of a particular task, but they misunderstand what they're supposed to do. If you find out about the misunderstanding right away, you can make corrections. If days go by with no corrections, you'll have wasted valuable time and money on a project that has to be restarted from scratch.

To avoid this problem, spot check the work, particularly with new team members, and do it early in the project. Better yet, have someone who has worked with you a long time check the new person's work so you don't have to. Once you know your requests are interpreted correctly, step back and let your team members do their jobs.

Problems with new employees can also be avoided by creating simplified processes and documenting how different procedures are done. Everyone should have a specific set of jobs to do, and everything they do should be mapped out clearly. If that employee quits tomorrow, a replacement should be able to step in and do the job easily, with little training. Your business should run like a well-oiled machine.

A successful real estate investor knows how to let people do their jobs – without losing control of the business.

15

Be united in public.
Disagree in private.

One of the biggest mistakes business partners make is to disagree in public. Public disagreement is a visible sign of weakness. In real estate in particular, this practice can be devastating because it affects the tone of your negotiations.

If you and your partner are in the middle of negotiating a deal on a property, the last thing you want is for the buyer or seller – whichever the case may be – to think you and your partner can be divided. If you disagree with each other in front of the other party, that's exactly what will happen. Now the other person knows a better deal will result by playing you and your partner against each other.

I knew an investor who wanted to purchase a piece of land with his partner. They had different ideas about what they were looking for, and unfortunately they didn't take the time to iron out these discrepancies before they went into the land deal. It didn't take the seller long to figure that out, particularly when the first investor hesitated and his partner said to him, in front of the seller, "No, I think we should check this out. It's a better deal than you think."

When the first investor indicated he was reluctant to move forward, the seller went behind his back and negotiated a deal with his partner. Big mistake for everyone. Not only did the partnership dissolve. It turned out the first investor was right to be cautious. The land wasn't worth what the partner thought. In the end, he lost a lot of money on the deal.

The lesson? If you are negotiating a real estate deal together with a partner, be sure you agree on all possible criteria before you talk to the third party. If questions arise, save them for a private discussion later with your partner. Don't show any sign of disagreement in front of a seller or buyer.

This applies not only to real estate transactions but also to any public discussion concerning your real estate business. If you have reason to disagree with an employee or team member, don't do so in front of others. It's a sign you're not in control, and others will use that against you.

When you talk privately with your partner, employees or team members, the opposite holds true. Be as honest as necessary. Don't hesitate to disagree. After all, you're the leader. It's your real estate investing business, and you're in charge. When others express concern, it's always a good idea to listen, but you have the final say about how your business is run. Disagree openly, whenever it's necessary, so you and your partners or employees don't stumble into a serious mistake.

Disagreement is often a necessary part of working with others on real estate transactions. Just remember to keep the disagreements private and present a united front in public.

16

Value your team.

Take charge of your success.

You won't succeed in real estate investing without a top-notch team working for you. To become a leading real estate investor, you need access to the best properties, the best research, the best analysis, the best networks… And you need to work on multiple high-end deals in several locations at once. You don't have time to do everything yourself. Your success will depend on those you bring on board to help you.

In any type of business, too many people make the mistake of becoming paranoid the moment they get into a leadership role. They want only "Yes" people under them. They want people working for them who don't threaten their own position. Their egos are too fragile to hire confident professionals with a track record of success.

What if this person tries to take over my business? or *What if I train this person, pay him and then he leaves to work for someone else?* These are the questions asked by business executives that lack the confidence to become true leaders in their industry. They are always afraid of the people who work under them. They refuse to put truly outstanding talent in charge of their projects.

Because they refuse to hire the best, these executives condemn themselves to mediocrity. They will never become outstanding leaders because they don't have the support they need. In real estate investing, the sky is the limit, but only if you have a genuine success team to propel you to the top.

Because your team is so important to your success, it's important that you continue to evaluate your team's performance and capabilities. The real estate investing business never sits still. You're always moving ahead – on to bigger and better deals. To become a leading investor, you need to recognize when it's time to move on and leave a team member behind.

If you've hired the best, it's sometimes hard to know when to move on. There's nothing wrong with the person's performance. They are the best at what they do. But are they the best for what you need now? The individuals that will help you the most when you first start out are not necessarily the same people that will help you when you move into bigger real estate deals.

You don't ever want a member of your team to limit what you can accomplish. They are supposed to propel you ahead, not hold you back. If a team member is limiting what you can accomplish, you need to move on, regardless of how well that person has performed the job.

Years ago, I worked with a loan officer who was the best at what he did. In five years of working for me, he made perhaps two mistakes. I couldn't have asked for better support. But as I became involved with bigger, more complex real estate transactions, I realized this loan officer was limiting my possibilities. It wasn't his fault. The company he worked for limited the number of loans they made available. I finally reached a point where I couldn't obtain the types of loans I needed. I had no choice: I had to move on and find a new loan officer.

This happens often to real estate investors. When they start purchasing multiple properties, they run into problems with loan officers who can't get them qualified on everything. It has nothing to do with the investor's financial situation. It's the result of the limited vision of that loan company.

If this happens to you, if someone keeps telling you they can't get you qualified on all the transactions you need to complete in order to build your business, don't assume you are the problem. You might just be working with the wrong person – even if that individual has been a great asset up to that point.

Don't ever make the mistake of sticking with an individual or a process, just because things are working and your business is successful. This will be of particular concern when you first start to experience success. You'll be afraid that if you make any changes, you will lose your edge. Remember that the opposite holds true. If you don't keep things fresh and if you don't have the team in place to bring you to the next level, you'll never get there. You might maintain a modest success, but you'll never become a leading real estate investor.

In every situation where I left people behind, I always did better. Moving ahead always expanded my vision and opened new possibilities. No matter how good your team is, there is always someone out there who is hungrier, with better ideas, better companies to back them and more contacts. Don't hold on to what's working when you need something better to reach the next level.

In short, hire the best, appreciate the value of your team, but know when it's time to move on. Remember that you alone are responsible for your success.

DON'T STOP WITH SUCCESS ...THINK BIGGEST

The key to becoming a successful real estate agent is to think biggest – without overlooking the small deals that can earn you a profit.

Too many investors limit their thinking and are afraid to try new types of investment deals. Because they are comfortable selling new homes, for example, they miss opportunities in land acquisitions. Because they are used to buying and selling condos, they are reluctant to jump into apartment buildings.

For every real estate investor that hesitates to venture out, there's another that tries to move up too quickly. New investors who haven't gotten their feet wet try to become involved in large-scale commercial projects or luxury real estate. Because they try to move too far too quickly, they sabotage their career from the start.

Keep your goals ambitious but don't overlook the opportunity to profit from small deals. Learn the craft. Stick to the basics. Build a foundation. Be realistic. Then when you're ready, get out there and jump into everything.

V. STAY ON FIRE

17

Act cool.

Give it your all.

Have you ever seen the movie *Cool Hand Luke*? If you haven't you should. No matter what happens, this guy plays it cool, and as a real estate investor, that's how you need to act. Always be cool. Always keep a calm bearing. Don't wear your emotions for everyone to see.

You want everyone to believe success comes easily to you; that you could make money in your sleep. That's how you'll get clients to invest with you. They try real estate investing and see how complicated it is. Suddenly you come along and make everything look easy. It's a given they'll want to invest with you. That's how you'll become a leading investor, by leading others to great success.

Everyone wants to be with someone who can show them how easy it is to make money. Think about it. If you needed help with something, who would you go to? The person who struggles just as you do? Or the person who makes it seem simple?

If you experience technical problems with your computer, would you ask for help from someone who's in the middle of throwing their computer out the window? Or would you go to the technophile who could have everything up and running again in a few simple steps?

If you were depressed, would you ask help from someone struggling with depression? Or would you talk to someone upbeat, someone who could lift you out of your depression?

It's the same with real estate investing. If you were desperate to make money, would you want to work with an investor that always seems stressed out? If you're in a tough spot now, why would you want this person's help? If this investor is always stressed, working together will not help alleviate your stress.

To be a successful real estate investor, you need to look the part. Everyone has an image of what a successful investor looks like, and you need to fit that image or they will be reluctant to invest with you. People want to associate with someone who can elevate them to the next level – someone who is there already, living their dreams; someone that can help them reach that point. They don't want to work with someone who looks the same or worse than they feel right now.

I was listening to some movers talk one time as they were packing up my furniture on the moving van. One of them was begging the other to set up a meeting with his buddy who could offer a job that paid $12 an hour. He went on about how, with that kind of pay, he could finally buy a house. Earning $12 an hour might not sound like a lot, but for someone who was paid $7 an hour as a mover, that was the next step up. He wanted to meet with someone who could bring him to that level.

For someone earning $100,000 a year, their next step up is a Rolex or Lamborghini. They want to associate with people at that level, people who can help them get there. Meanwhile, the people at that level are looking at people that own two Aston Martins, a Ferrari and a 5,000-square-foot home with an infinity pool overlooking the city. For the person that already owns those possessions, they want to be around the person with the Learjet.

People always want to associate with the person who's a step higher. Regardless of where you are in relation to others, if you want to be a successful real estate investor with lots of clients, you need to fit the part. Always let them believe you are the person that can bring them to the next level.

It's more than an act, though. To play this role, you have to work harder than those around you. Don't start believing your own act. You won't get ahead just by acting cool. Act like the person who has everything, but work like the person who is starving. Give it everything you've got. Act hungry – and don't confuse that with desperation or weakness. It's not about that. It's about having a fire lit under you.

Too many people mistake initiative for desperation, and confidence for arrogance. You have to know the difference not only in terms of your own behavior, but also with people you hire to work for you. You want the hungriest people on your team. You want people who will give it everything, who will work like they have a fire lit under them. You want confidence. You want initiative.

If you can't tell the difference in other people, take a long look at yourself, because you're probably not as confident and hungry as you need to be.

To be successful, you have to play the part. You have to act cool. Make people believe that successful real estate investing comes easily to you, that it's as natural as breathing. But don't be fooled into believing that's enough. You won't get anywhere unless you're prepared to work harder than everyone else.

18

Learn patience.
Don't become lazy.

Someone once told me that overnight success takes 15 years. That's not always the case – for some it happens sooner, for others it takes longer – but the point is well taken. What this means is that when success comes, it looks as if it happened overnight. It didn't. It was the result of intensive work over a period of time and of lessons learned from every mistake.

If you treat real estate investing as a get-rich-quick scheme, you won't experience lasting success. You won't become a great investor. True success requires time and effort. Patience.

Don't confuse patience with complacency, however. Success takes time but you have to know how and when to push ahead. Don't allow yourself to be stuck in one place. Don't become lazy.

A 65-year-old real estate broker was asked, "How do you continue to make money at this age?"

His response: "I continue to knock on doors."

This is excellent advice for any real estate investor. Keep knocking on doors, and you'll find success. When you find it, don't stop knocking. Never stop doing the activities that brought you success. That's the difference between success on a small scale and huge success. A leading real estate investor never stops doing the work.

Always stick to the basics. Remember what got you there. Becoming successful doesn't mean you can become lazy. You don't know how long your success will last unless you keep trying for something bigger and keep the momentum going. Don't stop doing the research that brought you success. Don't stop reading newspapers, cold calling, knocking on doors. Don't allow yourself to get comfortable.

If you stop, you'll lose your momentum. You'll never achieve anything bigger. You might even lose what you've got. Then you'll be broke and you'll have to start over from scratch… if your ego lets you.

Success doesn't happen overnight. Be patient. When success comes your way, keep it going. Don't become lazy.

19

Think positively.

Have an exit strategy.

Overnight success happens rarely, but you need to be ready for it when it does happen. Otherwise you will miss opportunities. If you're not prepared for things to go well, and then they do go well, you won't react quickly enough to maximize the results. You'll end up earning less than you might have earned. You can turn one success into many, as long as you're ready to move on each opportunity. If you assume the worst or maintain low expectations, that will never happen.

Always think positively when you go into a transaction or when you look at an opportunity. You might not make it big on any one transaction, but you should always look at each deal as if this is the one that puts you over the top. You'll have a greater chance of success this way, and you'll also be ready to turn one success into many.

Though you should approach every project as if it will lead to great success, you also need an exit strategy, just in case things don't work out. Even when you have a "guaranteed" success, sometimes deals fall apart at the last minute, for reasons you can't predict. If a transaction falls through, that's less important than how you react. If you have an exit strategy, you'll be able to move quickly on to the next project without negative fallout from the deal that fell apart.

Imagine you're selling a piece of land. The buyer offers $245,000, and you're going to use that money to finance several other deals. What happens if the buyer doesn't receive the financing he expected? How will that affect your other deals?

If you structured the contracts so you have to close the day after your land sale, you'll be in trouble when the buyer has to back out at the last minute – unless you have another way to cover the costs of the properties you are buying. If you do, then you're fine. Always have a way to cover all the transactions to which you're committed.

Now imagine you're buying a piece of land and you need to conduct more research to be sure it's what you want. Put a 40-day due diligence clause into the contract. That way, if you find out it's not really what you want, you can exit without losing your money. Always have a way to move on.

Do you know people who put everything they've got into one company or one type of job? They don't think about what will happen if the company or industry goes under. What are they going to do if that happens? Live on unemployment? For how long? Think about the dot com craze. So many people put everything they had into the market. Some still haven't recovered their losses.

It's the same with real estate investing. If one investment doesn't work out, what else do you have going that will help you sustain your future and move toward your goals?

If you're doing multiple deals and one doesn't work out, have another one you can go into the very next day. If you have $10,000 to invest, for example, and you find three investments with a $10,000 buy-in option, start moving forward with the first deal while you research the other two. That way, if the first investment doesn't go through, you will be ready to move on the other two. Always have an exit strategy.

Let's say you're getting ready to invest in a new home that requires $2,500 earnest money. You invest that money while you wait six to seven months for the home to be built. If, during that time, the value of the home doesn't increase the way you anticipated, walk away. You'll lose your earnest money but you won't lose by taking on a new home that isn't profitable. By walking away, you have more to gain than lose.

When you buy pieces of land, hoping to sell the land or bring in a new home development, take advantage of the 45-day due diligence period to see how well the land will sell. You're not selling it yet, because you don't own it until the deal closes. But you can make inquiries, as long as you disclose to any prospective buyers that the land sale is subject to closing on your contract. If you don't find the interest in the property you expected, you can cancel and typically have your earnest money refunded.

Is it contradictory to think positively while creating an exit strategy? No. You can have high expectations and still be realistic. Both strategies give you a way to maximize your outcome, regardless of what transpires. Keep your expectations high to maximize your success. Put an exit strategy in place to minimize your risk. Be prepared to soar but always land on your feet.

20

Have a source of inspiration. And be one.

To be a successful real estate investor, you need to surround yourself with people wealthier than you or more knowledgeable in the business. These people will never tell you something can't be done. They will always inspire you to new levels of success. You'll see there is no limit to what you can accomplish.

When I first started working for a real estate company, one of the brokers sold five to six properties each month. I assumed that was the average. I had no idea most people in the firm sold only two to three properties a year.

Being naïve proved to be an advantage. Because I thought I needed to sell as many properties as this top broker, I modeled myself after him. I kept pushing myself harder. He inspired me to keep doing better. At the end of my first year, I won the Rookie of the Year award because I sold more properties than anyone.

It's best to come into real estate investing without preconceived ideas or attitudes that will stand in your way. You're more apt to listen and to believe you can accomplish whatever you want. When you surround yourself with successful people, they make things seem so easy you develop a positive mindset.

Even though things might be difficult when you start out, these people will encourage you to keep trying. They will inspire you to do better. You'll realize the tough period you go through is something all new real estate agents experience. You'll be less likely to become discouraged.

When you surround yourself with successful people, you taste the good life before you get there. You see the end result and you know that if you keep trying, you'll be exactly where they are, perhaps even further. By continually seeing what's possible, you'll become even more eager to get there quickly.

When you do succeed, be conscious of the effect you have on others just starting out. Carry yourself well and don't develop a superior attitude. Remember where you came from and help people who want to be helped. You can be a source of inspiration.

If you know someone is hungry to learn and succeed, that's probably someone you want to partner with. Everyone grows older daily. Even if you're doing well now, if you have a younger person willing to work hard, you want to start a relationship with that person now, at the beginning of their success. If you wait until they've made it, they won't need to partner with you.

Always remember that teams earn more money than individuals. One person can only do so much, but as a team, you will experience twice the success. You can each work to your strengths. One of you might be good at interacting with people, while the other might have strong technical or financial skills. All that stands in the way of a good partnership is ego and greed. Set those aside, and there's no reason you can't succeed.

On your way up, partner with those above you, with people who can keep you inspired. When you achieve success, partner with people on their way up – people eager to learn, eager to let you inspire them to success.

VI. PUSH YOUR BOUNDARIES

21

Push your boundaries.
Not too far.

In my years of investing in real estate, I've noticed a pattern: Whenever I'm realistic, things work out. Whenever I'm not realistic, things also work out. What's the difference? The difference is that I earn much more when I'm *not* realistic.

If I know a project is worth $300,000, but I make the unrealistic determination to earn $7 million on it, I end up earning somewhere close to $3 million. Sure, I knew $7 million was impossible. But because I went for it, I earned much more than I would have earned had I approached the project realistically.

To be successful at real estate investing, you can't always think realistically. Sometimes you have to push your boundaries and think beyond what's realistic. Price is relative. Perception is everything. A piece of property is worth what a buyer is willing to pay. You sell it at that price. It's as simple as that. Don't sabotage the deal by continuing to question whether or not you're being realistic.

Push your boundaries – and don't question yourself when you succeed.

There is an exception to pushing your boundaries, and a savvy investor knows where to draw the line. Push where you can, but know when to hold back. If you're trying to have a property rezoned, for example, and the county tells you there is no way they will change the zoning, walk away. If you try to push, you'll be wasting your time and energy, when you could focus instead on a more promising project.

Before you push, know what your real boundaries are. But once those are set, be unrealistic about everything else you do. You'll get much further that way.

22

Think big.

Appreciate small deals.

If anything hurt my own success in the past, it was thinking too small. When you think big, you can accomplish so much more. This includes pushing boundaries and thinking unrealistically, but it's more than that. It also means moving out of your comfort zone.

If you start out buying and selling houses, don't limit yourself for too long. Move into new areas where you have no experience. Condos, land, apartment buildings… if you're afraid to venture into more complex real estate transactions, you'll never become truly successful. To become a leading investor, you have to be willing to jump in and learn.

At one time, I planned to go to law school. A man I was working with told me, "Why spend all that time in school to become an attorney, when you can go out instead, make a lot of money and then hire the best attorneys?" He was right. It pays more to think big.

What if there's a 50-acre piece of property for sale and the price is excellent, but you need only 30 acres? Will you pass up the opportunity? If you do, you're limiting yourself. Instead, you should buy the 50 acres and sell 20 at a higher profit. You'll earn back what you would have paid for the 30 and you'll have an additional profit. You won't get that by thinking small.

If a new home development is expected to do extremely well, but you buy only two properties because you're worried about trying to sell more than that, you're limiting yourself. If you can sell two, why couldn't you sell 20? What will you say when, six months down the road, the value of each home in that development jumps up by $100,000? You'll wish you had bought 20 homes instead of two.

If you're going to be a successful real estate investor, you need to recognize that you can sell property. That's what you do, after all. If you lack confidence, if you hesitate and are afraid you won't be able to sell, you're in the wrong business. That would be like a car mechanic being afraid to buy a car in case it breaks down. If you invest in property for a living, don't hesitate to buy a few more properties than you're comfortable with. As long as you're buying property for the right reasons, based on due diligence, it shouldn't matter whether you buy two or 20.

While you should continually move out of your comfort zone, that doesn't mean you should expect to become rich from every real estate transaction. Be realistic. Some deals are smaller than others. There's nothing wrong with that. If you need to earn $60,000 and you have an opportunity to sell a house for $15,000, sell four of them. Appreciate every opportunity that comes your way.

Too many new investors think they'll get rich from every single deal. That's not a mindset that leads to great success. If your mind is truly focused on the business, you shouldn't care whether you earn $20,000 or $200,000 on a deal. Every profit adds up.

If you want to become a leading investor, you learn to build your success from every opportunity. Don't go out and try to earn as much as possible from one deal. Make up your mind to turn a profit, however big or small, on every transaction. If all you net is

$5,000, that's still a profit. No one has ever taken a loss making a profit.

I was selling a house listed at $15,000 above market. I negotiated with a buyer who was willing to take it for $5,000 above market. I agreed to the sale. I could have held out for $15,000 above, but there was no guarantee. Instead, I took the profit. I might have earned more, but I also might have earned nothing. The best approach is to get your money while you can – legally, ethically, honestly. Don't hold out for greed. Greed doesn't lead to success.

If you're in this business to make the real money, to earn a steady half million every year, it doesn't matter if you don't profit much on one transaction. You'll make up for it on the next deal, as long as you keep the right frame of mind. It's when you let emotions and greed get in the way that you'll run into trouble. That destroys your business mentality. If you're going to fret over the small deals, you're in the wrong business.

You can do multiple small projects and still hit big. Bigger, in fact. You will always do better in multiples than in single projects. When you do a single project, no matter how big the project is, you're thinking small. You're limiting yourself. When you do multiple projects, you're thinking big.

If you have to choose between investing in one 52-unit apartment building and eight fourplexes, for example, you'll do better with the fourplexes. You can take your time improving each and selling them off one at a time, whereas with the apartment building, you have to finish improvements on the whole structure before you can sell it and turn a profit. You have more potential for growth with the smaller projects.

If you buy the fourplexes for $200,000 each, for example, there's a good chance that with improvements, you can sell them for $480,000 each. If you buy the apartment building for $2 million, you won't earn more than $3 million when you sell it. That's less down on the fourplexes for a higher profit, not to mention less risk, because your risk is spread across multiple projects. And, when you sell off one fourplex at a time, you'll have money to invest quickly in other projects – rather than waiting for the entire apartment building to be completed before you can raise cash for other investments.

Sometimes thinking big means appreciating small deals.

23

Innovate.

Don't reinvent.

Too many people become stuck in a certain way of doing business. We still have realtors in this business who like doing things the old way. Unfortunately, they are limited by their approach. Buyers want virtual tours now. They want pictures emailed to them. They buy property over the Internet. If you aren't up with the times, you won't be able to sell. You won't capture new business. You'll be left in the past.

You should always keep up with innovations in real estate. Follow what successful people are doing that's new and better. That's what I like to do. Find out who is the most successful and keep up with everything they're doing. There's a reason for their success.

How do you keep up? Read all the information you can get your hands on – every real estate investing article available. I receive newspapers and magazines from all over the country and I read articles online. I search constantly. I look for new information that can help me grow as a real estate investor. Out of two or three magazines, I might find only two pages of relevant information, but that will be enough to let me know what I need to do. The information might tell me what second homebuyers are looking at right now, or why condotels are hot, or why the resort market is growing in certain locations. This is how I gain knowledge.

If you don't like to read, you'll have to get over that. Anything that's worth doing is worth doing right. You won't have to read forever… just until you can afford to hire someone to read for you or to provide market analysis. Look at it this way: The more you read now, the more quickly you'll experience success, and the sooner you'll be able to hire someone to give you the information you need to remain competitive.

Though you won't go far in this business without staying on top of innovations, you also don't want to reinvent the wheel. Avoid the temptation to go out and do something off the wall that nobody else is doing, just because you want to be the first to come up with a great idea. Don't try to change society overnight. Change happens over time. Keep up with the changes, stay at the cutting edge, but don't go out and try to turn everything on its head. It's very doubtful one investor will revolutionize the entire real estate industry. Just be the best at what you do and keep up with the changes.

Also remember what got you there. Don't jeopardize everything that's going right just so you can stay ahead. I've run across too many investors that want to switch their area of focus to whatever is "hot." They switch from residential to commercial, or they jump into luxury sales. That's fine – after all, pushing your boundaries is important – but in the process they throw away everything that led to their success. They ignore their old clients, as if they're too good to help them now. They leave their network behind.

It reminds me of this barber who wanted to open a record studio. He took money out of his barbershop to finance the project. When the studio didn't do well, he looked for another project and pulled more money out of his barbershop. That scheme failed too, and he searched for another. He did this over and over, failing each time, until he finally decided to stick to barbering. Unfortunately, by the time he realized he needed to go back to the basics, he had taken so much money out of his barbershop that it went under. He lost everything.

That's the problem with get-rich-quick schemes. They take you too far away from the basics, from what works. In the process, your ego forces you to burn bridges that might have helped you later on. Before you throw away everything you have, think twice. Be careful who and what you exclude. Go out and improve, and stay on the cutting edge, but don't let the business that got you there fall by the wayside. When all other projects fail, you'll need that foundation to keep going.

24

Appreciate where you are.
Know when to leave.

When you first start out in real estate investment, you probably won't focus on large transactions. You might find yourself doing smaller deals, and that might go on for a while. Appreciate it. Make the most of it. As long as you're making a profit, you're moving ahead. It's important for you to learn the craft. You can't just rush into new areas without knowing what you're doing.

Don't always think you have to buy $600,000 homes. If all you can buy right now are $100,000 homes, then be the best $100,000 investor you can be. Don't keep grumbling that you hate working at this level. Be grateful.

This doesn't mean you need to get stuck at this level. You want to move up, to move out of your comfort zone. But take your time and do it right. Don't rush. Just because you think you can box, you don't want to get into the ring with Ali. Be the best at what you do, and you'll know when it's time to move on. You'll be ready.

I talked to an agent recently who received his license six months ago. He's sold 10 small properties, and now he thinks he's ready to move out on his own, to start his own agency. "He's not as smart as he wants everyone to think," this agent told me, referring to his boss. "I can be more successful than he is." While that might be true, it's doubtful this agent will succeed if he goes out on his own with so little experience. Not only does he not have the experience required for confidence, but he also has no idea of what it costs to run his own business. If he were truly smart, he would stay where he is for a while, until he really learns what he needs to know to succeed on his own.

That's the way real estate investing has become. Everyone wants to be an investor and wants overnight success. Everyone wants to rush into things too big for them to handle. Too many people get into this business because they want to deal in commercial properties or million-dollar homes. If they try to start there, they will fail. Why? Because they haven't learned the craft. They haven't learned to sell $100,000 homes first. It's by working small deals that you learn how to do the bigger deals right.

You learn confidence too. Have you ever been inside a million-dollar home? Are you comfortable engaging in business as usual when you walk through a luxury mansion? If you go into every million-dollar home with your jaw hanging on the floor, or with your eyes open wide, you won't project confidence. No one will want to do business with you. They won't trust you, because you seem overwhelmed. That's what happens when you get in over your head. Instead of rushing to success, you hurt your growth.

Start where you have to. Appreciate what you've got. Learn the craft. Just don't get too comfortable. Know when it's time to move on.

ABOUT

THE AUTHOR

In the five years since he formed Dolce & Deluca Investments, LLC, Carlos Redmond has invested over $250 million for his clients, who have earned double their investment on every real estate transaction. His client list consists of hotel presidents, attorneys, law enforcement officers, realtors, singers, actors, entertainment managers, union executives, bank vice presidents, judges, doctors, accountants and councilmen. He has brokered their investments in homes, land, condos, town homes, mid-rises and high-rises.

Known for his tireless research and in-depth market knowledge, Mr. Redmond was hired by the District Attorney's office to broker their relocation and was appointed by the court to sell a $3 million piece of land. Top builders routinely offer him first bid on new properties and homes that fall out of escrow.

Mr. Redmond continues to design new real estate investment strategies and methods. Rather than take a standard investment package off the shelf, he believes in tailoring each investment to his individual clients' needs. To show confidence in his recommendations, he has invested his money exactly where he advises his clients to invest.

An author of real estate investment books, including *The Art of Deals & Dreams*, and workshop materials for beginners, Mr. Redmond has been asked to teach classes in real estate investing, to write articles and to give radio interviews locally and nationally.

At a young age, Mr. Redmond learned to create opportunities for himself, and he enjoys sharing his insights with others. He believes anyone with the right outlook and willingness to learn can succeed in real estate investing. There are no limits except those people create in their minds.

Before forming Dolce & Deluca Investments, LLC, Mr. Redmond worked in the real estate section at the District Attorney's office. He later became top salesman at a Las Vegas real estate agency. Mr. Redmond is licensed as a real estate broker in Arizona, Colorado, D.C., Florida, Georgia, Idaho, Massachusetts, Nevada, New Mexico, New York, South Carolina, Virginia and Washington. He has licenses pending in California, Illinois, North Carolina, Oregon and Utah.

www.ingramcontent.com/pod-product-compliance
Lightning Source LLC
Chambersburg PA
CBHW060611200326
41521CB00007B/740